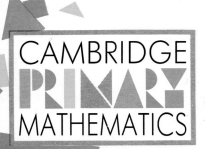

CAMBRIDGE PRIMARY MATHEMATICS

MODULE SIX
BOOK 2

KU-589-601

Roy Edwards
Mary Edwards
Alan Ward

Cambridge University Press
Cambridge
New York   Port Chester
Melbourne   Sydney

Published by the Press Syndicate of the University of Cambridge
The Pitt Building, Trumpington Street, Cambridge CB2 1RP
40 West 20th Street, New York, NY 10011, USA
10 Stamford Road, Oakleigh, Melbourne 3166, Australia

First published 1990

Printed in Great Britain by Scotprint Ltd, Musselburgh

British Library cataloguing in publication data
Edwards, Roy, *1931–*
Cambridge primary mathematics.
Module 6. Bk. 2
1. Mathematics
I. Title II. Edwards, Mary, *1936–* III. Ward, Alan, *1932–*
510

ISBN 0 521 36722 0

The authors and publishers would like to thank the many schools
and individuals who have commented on draft material for this
course. In particular, they would like to thank Anita Straker for
her contribution to the suggestions for work with computers,
Norma Anderson, Ronalyn Hargreaves (Hyndburn Ethnic
Minority Support Service) and John Hyland (Advisory Teacher
in Tameside).

Photographs are reproduced courtesy of:
front cover ZEFA; p 12 courtesy of the Post Office; p 18 AA Photo
Library; p 29 BFI Stills, Posters and Designs;
p 41 The Mansell Collection; p 43 British Antarctic Survey,
B. Herrod; pp 62, 88 Adrian Meredith photography; p 68 Barbados
Board of Tourism; pp 79, 81 Jacqueline Hirst; p 89 British Airways.

All other photographs by Graham Portlock.
The mathematical apparatus was kindly supplied by E J Arnold.

Designed by Chris McLeod

Illustrations by Chris Ryley
Diagrams by Oxprint
Children's illustrations by Jennifer Aguda, Robert Gilfillan
and Sarah Middleton

Knitting by Alice Bull

Contents

Number 9

In the reign of Queen Elizabeth I there were knitting schools where poor people were trained to knit. This was to help them to earn a living.

A

The blue section of the scarf has 20 rows.

1 $\frac{1}{4}$ of this section is ☐ rows.

2 $\frac{3}{4}$ of it is ☐ rows.

3 $\frac{1}{2}$ of it is ☐ rows.

There are 20 rows in the pink and red section.

4 $\frac{1}{5}$ of this section is ☐ rows.

5 $\frac{2}{5}$ of it is ☐ rows.

6 $\frac{4}{5}$ of it is ☐ rows.

7 $\frac{3}{5}$ of it is ☐ rows.

The green and yellow section has 30 rows.

8 $\frac{1}{3}$ of the section is ☐ rows.

9 $\frac{2}{3}$ of it is ☐ rows.

Let's investigate

Plan 12 rows of knitting.
Colour $\frac{1}{6}$ green, $\frac{1}{2}$ blue and $\frac{1}{3}$ yellow.
Plan and colour some more fraction patterns
for 12 rows of knitting.

B

There are 40 rows in the brown and black section.

1 $\frac{1}{10}$ of this section is ☐ rows.

2 $\frac{3}{10}$ of it is ☐ rows.

3 $\frac{7}{10}$ of it is ☐ rows.

4 $\frac{9}{10}$ of it is ☐ rows.

5 8 rows is $\frac{☐}{10}$ of it.

Look at the blue section
It has 48 rows.

6 $\frac{1}{6}$ of the section is ☐ rows.

7 $\frac{4}{6}$ of it is ☐ rows.

8 $\frac{2}{6}$ of it is ☐ rows.

9 $\frac{5}{6}$ of it is ☐ rows.

10 $\frac{1}{2}$ of it is ☐ rows.

The red and yellow section has 48 rows.

11 $\frac{1}{8}$ of the section is ☐ rows.

12 $\frac{3}{8}$ of it is ☐ rows.

13 $\frac{7}{8}$ of it is ☐ rows.

14 $\frac{5}{8}$ of it is ☐ rows.

15 12 rows is $\frac{☐}{8}$ of it.

6

Let's investigate

Two sections of the scarf have the same number of rows.
One section is coloured in $\frac{1}{5}$s, the other in $\frac{1}{10}$s.
How many rows could there be in each section?
Find different ways to do it.
Record your answers.

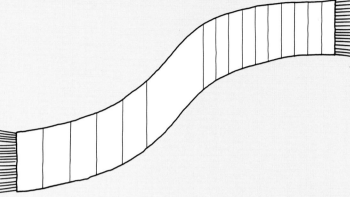

C Let's investigate

Design a knitted scarf for a small teddy bear.
It must be 100 rows long.
Choose 2 or 3 different fraction sections of colour for it.
They need not be the same as the picture.
Make the rest of the scarf grey.

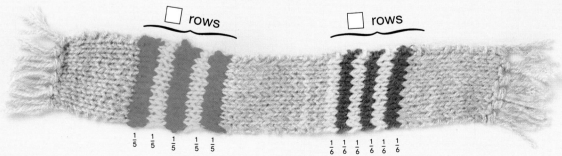

☐ rows   ☐ rows

$\frac{1}{5}$ $\frac{1}{5}$ $\frac{1}{5}$ $\frac{1}{5}$ $\frac{1}{5}$ $\frac{1}{6}$ $\frac{1}{6}$ $\frac{1}{6}$ $\frac{1}{6}$ $\frac{1}{6}$ $\frac{1}{6}$

Draw a plan of the scarf.
Write the number of rows and fractions for each colour section,
and the number of rows of grey knitting in the scarf.

Time 2

A

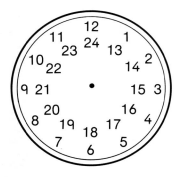

The hour hand goes round the clock twice in 24 hours.

Midnight is 00:00
Midday is   12:00

Copy these charts.
Write the 24 hour clock times.

1
10 a.m.	
11 a.m.	
noon	
1 p.m.	13:00
2 p.m.	

2
10 p.m.	
11 p.m.	
midnight	00:00
1 a.m.	01:00
2 a.m.	

Mrs Lee - Dayplan

05:00	Start work and sort letters.
07:00	Go out on 1st round.
09:30	Go back for more letters.
11:00	Go out on 2nd round.
13:00	Finish work.
13:15	Home for lunch.

3 Show the times for the day plan on clock faces.

4 How long does the first round take?

5 How long does the second round take?

Use a clock to help you.

6 How many hours does the postwoman work altogether?

8

The first post boxes were put up in the 1850s. Before this people had to take their letters to the post office to post them.

The times when letters will be collected are shown on each post box. Change these collection times to a.m. or p.m. times.

7

Collections

10:15
14:30
17:00
20:15

Change these collection times to 24 hour clock times.

8

Collections

8:00 a.m.
12:00 noon
3:00 p.m.
5:15 p.m.

9

Collections

7:45 a.m.
11:30 a.m.
2:15 p.m.
4:45 p.m.

Let's investigate

Plan collection times for two more post boxes.
Each one must start with a different time.
Write them as 24 hour clock times.
Write them again as a.m. or p.m. times.

B

Follow the arrows.
Show these times on clock faces.

The Travelling Post Office or T.P.O. is a special mail train. While it is travelling, the mail on board is sorted for the towns and cities on its route.

1 16:45

The 1st class letter is posted in Lancaster.

↓

2 17:00

The letter is collected from the post box.

↓

3 17:30

It arrives at the Post Office for sorting.

↓

4 21:10

The 1st class letters leave Lancaster on the T.P.O.

↓

5 21:52

The train arrives at Preston. The London mail is taken off.

↓

6 22:53

The letter leaves Preston on the T.P.O. for London. →

10 07:45

The postman delivers the letter.

↑

9 03:10

The letter arrives in London.

↑

8 00:22

The train leaves Crewe.

↑

7 23:52

The train stops at Crewe.

10

The first postage stamps were sold on 1st May 1840. They were the Penny Blacks. Before then a lot of the mail was paid for when it arrived and people often cheated the Post Office.

11 How long is the time from when the letter is collected to when it leaves Lancaster?

12 How long does the journey take from Lancaster to Preston?

13 How many minutes does the letter wait at Preston?

14 How long does the journey take from Preston to Crewe?

15 How long does the T.P.O. wait at Crewe?

16 How long does the journey take from Preston to London?

17 How many hours is it from when the letter is posted to when it is delivered?

Let's investigate

Work with a partner and write pairs of 24 hour clock times. They must be 12 hours apart like these.

               + 12 hours

05:30 ⟶ 17:30

Write or draw what you are usually doing at each of the times you choose.

C

There is a Post Office
underground railway
below the streets of London.
The trains only carry mail
and have no drivers.
More than ten million bags of
mail are carried on it each year.

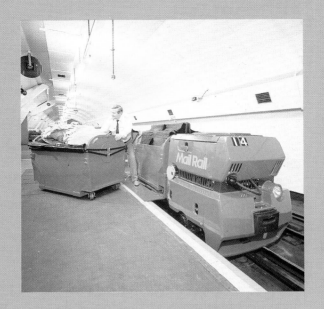

The railway is open from 08:00 on Monday to 20:30 on Saturday.
It is closed on Sundays.
There is a 2 hour break every working day for maintenance work.

1. How many hours each week does the railway run?

2. How many hours a week is it closed?

3. How could you check that your last two answers are correct?

At peak periods trains pass through the stations every 4 minutes.
Write the times for the next eight trains. Use 24 hour clock times.

4. 12:52 ⟶ 12:56 ⟶

5. 23:54 ⟶

6. If a train passed through the station at 20:33, how many
more would pass that way before 21:20?

Let's investigate

If trains always pass through a station at regular intervals, how
many different timetables can you plan for them?
Each timetable must start at 23:30 and finish exactly 1 hour later.

Co-ordinates

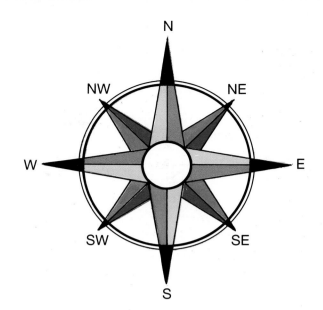

A

1 Copy the grid for Rushby.
The co-ordinates of the café
are (4,2).

Show these places
on your grid.

2 Church (8,8)

3 Gift shop (8,6)

4 Car park (2,4)

5 Swimming pool
(8,2)

6 Theatre (2,8)

7 Museum (6,8)

8 Bus station
(6,4)

9 Supermarket
(6,6)

10 Garage (4,6)

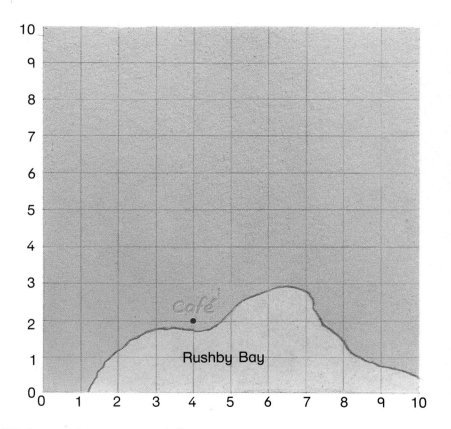

11 Which place is NE from the car park?

12 Write the directions of three places from the museum.

13 Write the directions of three places from the bus station.

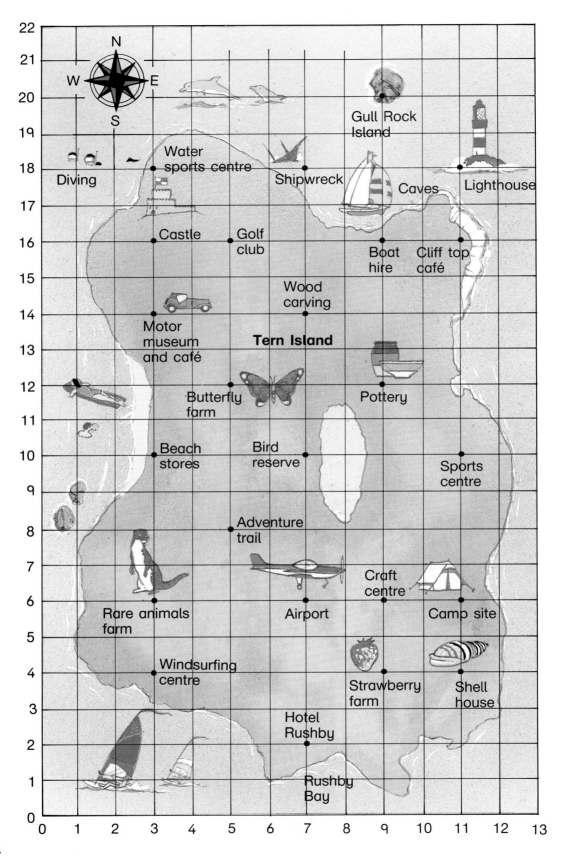

22
21
20
19
18
17
16
15
14
13
12
11
10
9
8
7
6
5
4
3
2
1
0

N
W   E
S

Diving

Water sports centre

Shipwreck

Gull Rock Island

Caves   Lighthouse

Castle   Golf club

Boat hire   Cliff top café

Wood carving

Motor museum and café

Tern Island

Butterfly farm

Pottery

Beach stores

Bird reserve

Sports centre

Adventure trail

Rare animals farm

Airport

Craft centre

Camp site

Windsurfing centre

Strawberry farm

Shell house

Hotel Rushby

Rushby Bay

0   1   2   3   4   5   6   7   8   9   10   11   12   13

Write the co-ordinates of these places.

14 Butterfly farm (☐ , ☐)   **15** Pottery   **16** Lighthouse

17 Shipwreck   **18** Airport   **19** Gull Rock Island

20 Shell house

Let's investigate

Find four places on the map that make a square.
Write their co-ordinates in order and give
the directions from each point to the next.

B Write the names and co-ordinates of places you might visit on the island if you were interested in these things.

There may be more than one place to visit each time.

1 Cliff walking

2 Aeroplanes

3 Swimming and sunbathing

4 Windsurfing

5 Craft

6 Bird watching

7 Diving

8 History

9 Visiting islands and lighthouses

10 Sport

11 Museums

12 Wildlife

13 Plan some 3-day tours from the hotel.
Arrange to visit three different places each day.
Write your plans giving co-ordinates and directions
from one place to the next.

Day 1   Hotel (7,2) ⟶ (N) Bird reserve (7,10) ⟶

Day 2   Hotel (7,2) ⟶

Day 3   Hotel (7,2) ⟶

Try this island word search.
Read the co-ordinates to find the names of islands.

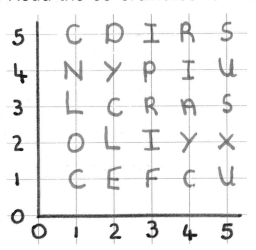

14	(1,1) (1,2) (4,5) (3,1) (5,4)
15	(1,5) (4,2) (3,4) (3,3) (5,1) (5,3)
16	(3,5) (4,1) (2,1) (1,3) (4,3) (1,4) (2,5)
17	(5,5) (4,4) (1,5) (3,2) (2,2) (2,4)
18	Find the islands on a map of the world.

Use this island search grid.
Write the co-ordinates of these Scottish islands.

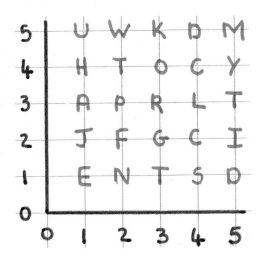

19	Mull
20	Skye
21	Arran
22	Iona
23	Find the islands on a map of Britain.

Let's investigate

Use an atlas or map of the world.
Choose four islands and make an island search of your own.
Write the co-ordinates of the letters.
Ask a friend to find the four names.

C

1 Copy this grid and
join the co-ordinates.

$(1,1) \longrightarrow (1,3) \longrightarrow (3,5) \longrightarrow (5,5)$
$\longrightarrow (5,3) \longrightarrow (3,1) \longrightarrow (1,1)$

What shape have you made?

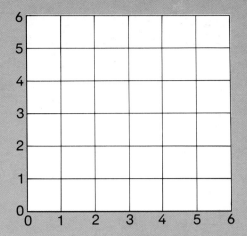

2 Reverse all the co-ordinate numbers like this.

$(1,1) \longrightarrow (3,1) \longrightarrow (\blacksquare,\blacksquare) \longrightarrow (\blacksquare,\blacksquare) \longrightarrow (\blacksquare,\blacksquare) \longrightarrow (\blacksquare,\blacksquare)$
$\longrightarrow (\blacksquare,\blacksquare)$

Draw another grid and join the new co-ordinates.
Do you make the same shape?

3 Draw another grid and join these co-ordinates.

$(0,0) \longrightarrow (0,1) \longrightarrow (1,1) \longrightarrow (1,0)$
$\longrightarrow (0,0)$

4 Reverse the co-ordinates.
Join them on a grid.
What shape have you made now?

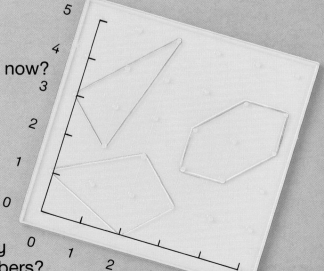

Let's investigate

Do other co-ordinate shapes stay
the same if you reverse the numbers?
Record your findings on a grid.

17

Number 10

A

Chart 1 on the clipboard shows a
traffic count for a busy road.

1 Which was the busiest day?

2 Why do you think it was the busiest?

3 Copy chart 1.
Round each number to the nearest thousand.

3637 ⟶ 4000
2086 ⟶

4 Copy chart 2.
Find the total number of vehicles
for each pair of days.
Write these on your chart.

5 Add the rounded numbers from chart 1
for each pair of days.
Write these totals on chart 2.

6 Which rounded total is closest to its real total?

7 Write numerals for Friday's traffic.

Cars	Two thousand four hundred and fifty-one
Vans and lorries	One thousand five hundred and twenty-nine
Coaches	Two hundred and eighty-three
Motor bikes	One hundred and thirty

Chart 1.

Traffic Count

Day	Vehicles	Numbers rounded to nearest thousand
Monday	3637	4000
Tuesday	2086	
Wednesday	1972	
Thursday	2714	
Friday	4393	

Chart 2.

	Total number of vehicles	Totals of Rounded Numbers
Monday } Tuesday }		
Tuesday } Wednesday }		
Wednesday } Thursday }		
Thursday } Friday }		

Let's investigate

Plan a traffic survey near your school.
What is the purpose of your survey?
What kinds of traffic will you count?
How will you record the numbers?
When will you carry out your survey?
What safety rules will you make?

 B

This chart shows the number
of child pedestrians involved
in road accidents in one year.

Jan	1574
Feb	1604
Mar	1910
Apr	1995
May	2265
June	2034
July	1810
August	1614
Sept	1752
Oct	1952
Nov	1667
Dec	1469

Find the total for
each group of months.

1 January, February and March

2 April, May and June

3 July, August and September

4 October, November and December

5 Which groups of months have the lowest total?

6 Which group of months has the highest total?
Why do you think this is?

Write in words the numbers for these months.

7 May   **8** June   **9** July   **10** August

20

Predict which pairs of numbers in the chart add up to these totals. The numbers must be next to each other.

11 4299   **12** 3178   **13** 3366   **14** 3704

15 3136   **16** 3514   **17** 4260   **18** 3619

19 Check your answers. How many did you predict correctly?

20 Round each month-number to the nearest 100.

21 If all the months on the chart are rounded to the nearest thousand, which is the odd one out?

Put in the missing sign > or <.

22 1910 ☐ 1995   **23** 1574 ☐ 1469   **24** 1604 ☐ 1614

25 What is the approximate total for November, December and January?

Let's investigate

☐ + ☐

When the missing numbers are rounded they add up to 5000.

Find some pairs of numbers that would fit in the boxes.
Choose some numbers that round up and some that round down.

C

The New Beaver

SALES FIGURES

January	6730
February	5321
March	7810
April	5609
May	7395

Estimate, by rounding, which pairs of numbers on the chart make these approximate totals.

1 Twelve thousand

2 Thirteen thousand

3 Fourteen thousand

4 Fifteen thousand

Let's investigate

Round these sales figures to the nearest thousand.
Predict which pair will give an approximate total nearest to the true one.
Predict which pair will give an approximate total furthest away from the true one?
Why did you choose these pairs of numbers?
Check to see whether you were right.

SALES
2910
4670
3850
2740

Work with a friend and choose some other numbers to do this with.

Look at the graph.
What was the temperature
at these times?

Graph of Monday's temperature

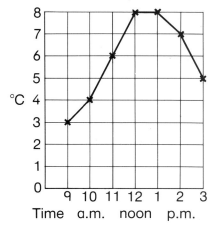

| 1 | 9 a.m. | 2 | 11 a.m. | 3 | 1 p.m. |

What time were these temperatures?

| 4 | 4 °C | 5 | 5 °C | 6 | 7 °C |

| 7 | How long was the temperature 8 °C? |

What was the increase in temperature between these times?

| 8 | 9 a.m. and 11 a.m. | 9 | 10 a.m. and 12 noon |

| 10 | 9 a.m. and 12 noon |

| 11 | How long did the children record the temperature for? |

23

Tuesday's temperatures

Time	9 a.m.	10 am	11 am	12 noon	1 p.m.	2 p.m.	3 p.m.
°C	3	5	6	9	8	4	2

12 Use the table. Draw a graph to show Tuesday's temperatures.

Let's investigate

When might a temperature graph
look like this?
Explain your answer.
How could you test it?

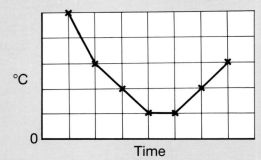

B

Graph of temperature

What was the temperature at these times?

1 6 a.m.   **2** 12 noon   **3** 2 p.m.   **4** 10 p.m.

5 How long was the temperature above zero?

6 How long was the temperature below zero?

7 Estimate the times when the temperature was 4 °C.

Estimate the temperature at these times

8 9 a.m.   **9** 3 p.m.   **10** 9 p.m.

11 Is the graph for winter or summer? How do you know?

24

12 Copy this graph.

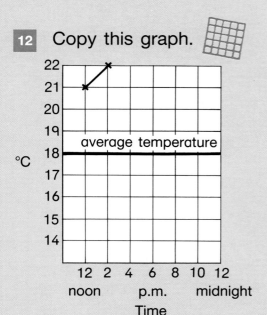

13 Show these temperatures on the graph.

12 noon	3 °C above average
2 p.m.	4 °C above average
4 p.m.	2 °C above average
6 p.m.	average
8 p.m.	2 °C below average
10 p.m.	3 °C below average
12 midnight	4 °C below average

14 Join the temperatures with straight lines.

15 Write 3 sentences about the graph.

Let's investigate

Decide which temperatures are for each month of the year. Choose a type of graph to show this data. Draw it. Explain your choice.

Average monthly temperatures in London

16 °C	4 °C	16 °C	5 °C
9 °C	5 °C	12 °C	6 °C
7 °C	18 °C	11 °C	15 °C

C Last week, Monday was hotter than Tuesday and Thursday. Tuesday was colder than Wednesday and Thursday. Wednesday was hotter than Monday. Friday was the coldest day.

1 Write the temperatures for each day.

2 Show them on a bar-line graph.

Last week's temperatures

15 °C 18 °C 20 °C
14 °C 17 °C

Let's investigate

Plan a way of finding out how fast water cools. Try it and record your results on a graph.

A

Julius Caesar and his Roman soldiers first came to Britain in 55 BC.

I	1		XXI	21
II	2		XXII	22
III	3		XXIII	23
IV	4		XXIV	24
V	5		XXV	25
VI	6		XXVI	26
VII	7		XXVII	27
VIII	8		XXVIII	28
IX	9		XXIX	29
X	10		XXX	30
XI	11		XXXV	35
XII	12		XL	40
XIII	13		XLV	45
XIV	14		L	50
XV	15		LV	55
XVI	16		LX	60
XVII	17		LXX	70
XVIII	18		LXXX	80
XIX	19		XC	90
XX	20		C	100

1 Write the numbers from 1 to 10 in Roman numerals.

What are these numbers?

2 XXII **3** XXVI

4 XXXV **5** XXXVIII

6 XLIII **7** LIX

8 LXIV **9** XCVI

Write these numbers in Roman numerals.

10 25 **11** 29

12 37 **13** 41

14 68 **15** 82

16 73 **17** 94

C is the Roman numeral for 100.
A century is written as C.
It is 100 years.
M is the Roman numeral for 1000.

C	CC	CCC	CD	D	DC
100	200	300	400	500	600

18 How did the Romans write 700?

19 How did they write 800?

What are these numbers?

20 CXII

21 CCXXV

22 CXXX

23 CCCL

24 DX

25 CDXXI

26 CCLIV

27 CCCX

28 DCXX

What years do these numerals show?

29 MCC

30 MCCC

31 MCCCXXX

32 MCXIII

33 MD

34 How will 900 be written?

Roman books were written on rolls of papyrus
or parchment. Each one was written by hand,
so there were not many copies of any book.

We do not use the Roman numbers. Our numbers were introduced to Europe by the Arabs about 700 years ago and were based on early Indian numbers.

The Arabic numbers looked something like this.

35 Which of our numerals did the Romans not have?

Our numbers make it easier to subtract. Try these.

36
3217
− 1153

37
4718
− 2429

38
5236
− 1715

39
7894
− 3498
---

40 3652 − 1734

41 7156 − 4362

42 3021 − 1121

43 7448 − 3519

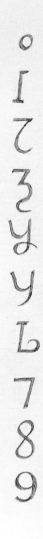

Let's investigate

CCXXV   CXII

Can you find a way to subtract these two Roman numbers? Explain to your teacher how you did it.

Try subtracting some other Roman numbers. Is it easier to subtract with our numbers? Explain why.

B The date when a TV programme was made often appears on the screen in Roman numerals.

This is a scene from the film 'Julius Caesar'.

The film was made in MCMLIII.

When were these programmes made?

1 MCMLXX   **2** MCMLXXX

3 MCMLX   **4** MCMLXXV

Write these dates in Roman numerals.

5 1980   **6** 1901   **7** 1956

8 1963   **9** 1991   **10** 1924

11 Write the date for the first year of the next century.

Old films are often shown on television.

12 How long ago was 'Julius Caesar' made?

How old will these films be in 2001?

13 MCMLXXIII   **14** MCMLXVI   **15** MCMLXXXIV

Let's investigate

Here are some Chinese numbers.

一	二	三	四	五	六	七	八	九	十	十一	十二
1	2	3	4	5	6	7	8	9	10	11	12

二十 三十
20   30

Work out what these might be in Chinese numbers.
40, 50, 60, 70, 80, 90
Work out what some other numbers might be.

29

C This number system has been made up.

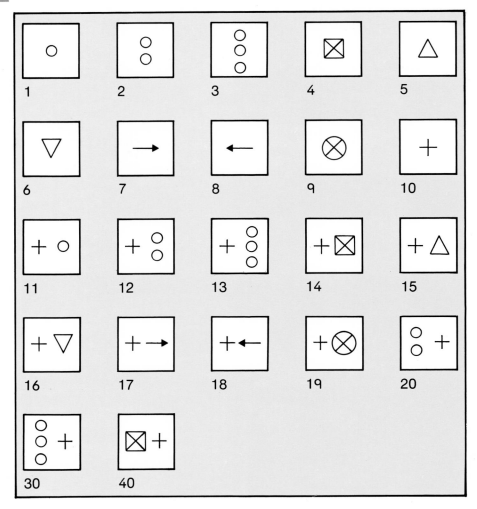

Think of a shape to show 100.
Use it and the shapes above to show these numbers.

| 1 | 140 | 2 | 230 | 3 | 260 | 4 | 463 | 5 | 801 | 6 | 999 |

Let's investigate

Plan a number system of your own.
Use it to write the numbers 1 to 30.

Angles 1

A The Greeks divided the circle into 360 parts.
They called each of the parts a degree.
We still measure angles in degrees today.

We write
360 degrees
as 360°.

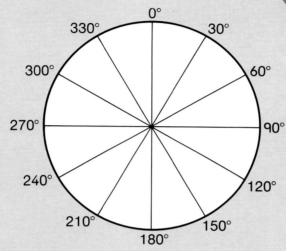

A full turn is 360°.

How many degrees are these angles?

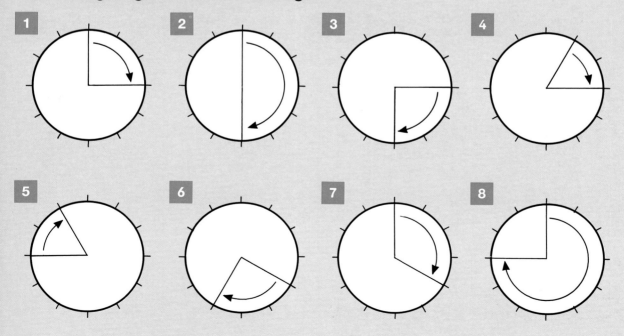

These protractors measure angles.

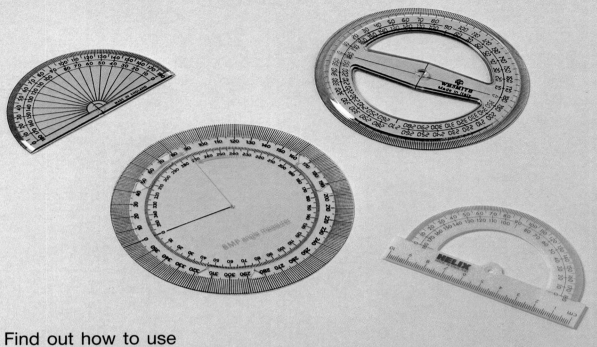

Find out how to use
your protractor.

Now use it to measure
these angles.

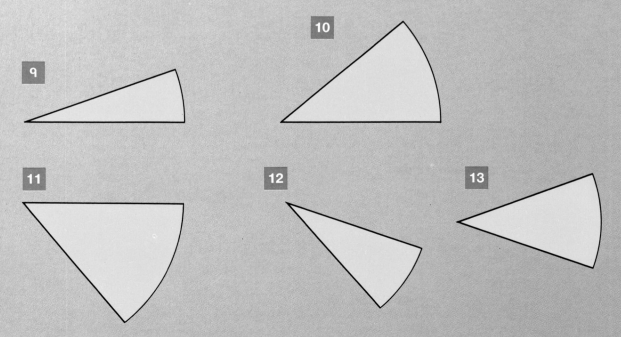

9

10

11

12

13

This colour spinner is divided
into 6 different colours.

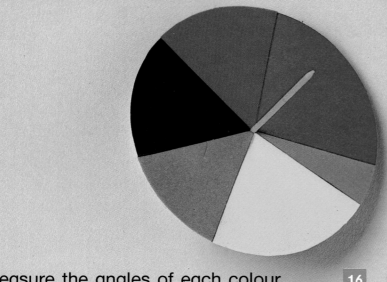

Measure the angles of each colour.

Let's investigate

Work with a friend. Measure and
draw pairs of angles and colour them.
Each pair must make a right-angle
when cut out and put together.

Explain how you could make
a spinner from your right-angles.

1 Measure the angles for each temperature on this weather dial.

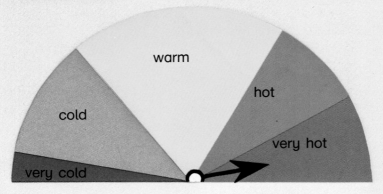

These are the parts of a wind dial.
Estimate the angle of each part.

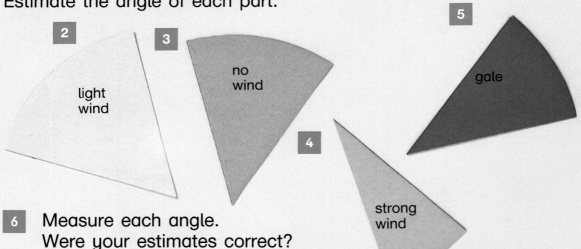

6 Measure each angle.
Were your estimates correct?

7 Make the angles. Cut them out.
Stick them on a piece of paper to make the dial.
What is the name for the angle that you have made?

Let's investigate

Show different ways to make a straight angle
using three angles each time.

This is a 'select-a-drink' dial.
You turn the dial clockwise until the drink arrow points to SELECT.
Always begin with the red arrow on SELECT for each new drink.

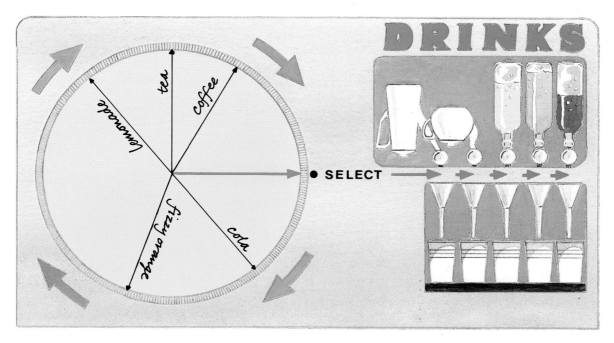

Measure the number of degrees you must move the dial through to get these drinks.

1 fizzy orange   **2** tea

3 lemonade   **4** cola   **5** coffee

Let's investigate

What do the angles at the centre of the select-a-drink dial add up to?

Do you think this will be the same for other dials?

Make one of your own. What do the angles add up to? Why do you think this is so?

Shape 3

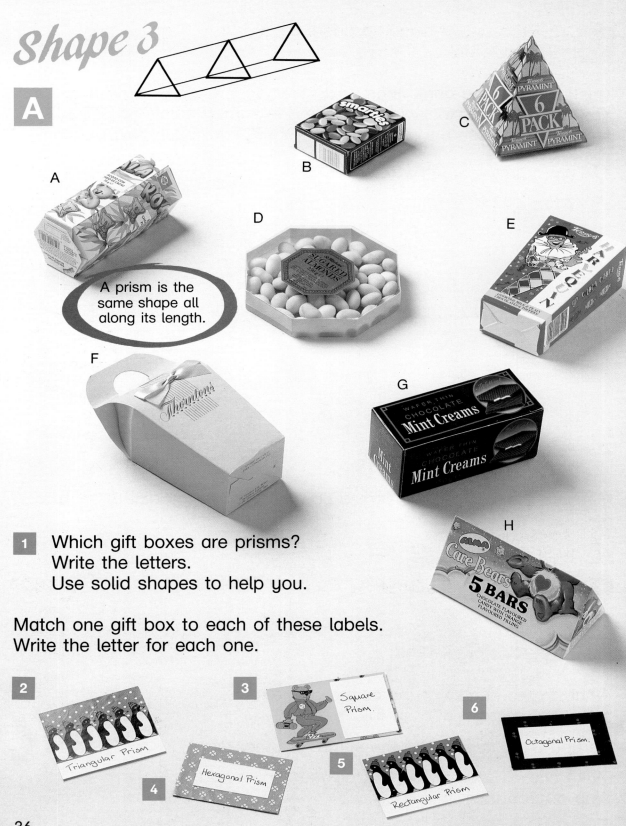

A prism is the same shape all along its length.

1 Which gift boxes are prisms?
Write the letters.
Use solid shapes to help you.

Match one gift box to each of these labels.
Write the letter for each one.

2 Triangular Prism

3 Square Prism.

4 Hexagonal Prism

5 Rectangular Prism

6 Octagonal Prism.

7 Draw this net on squared paper.
Draw some patterns on it.
Cut it out carefully.
Fold it to make a prism.

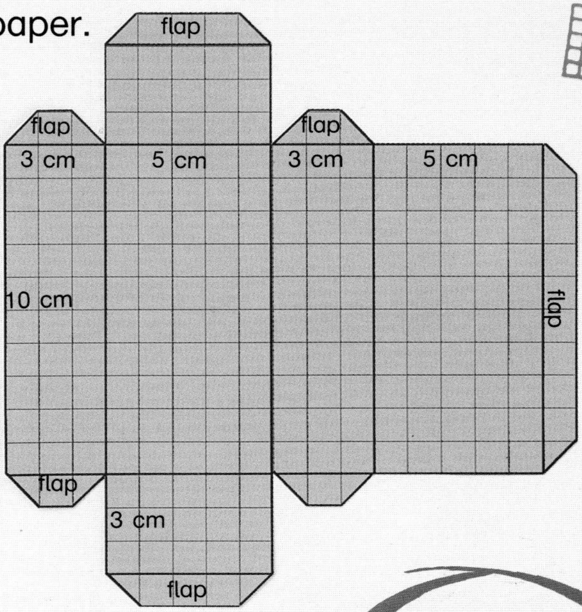

flap

flap   flap
3 cm   5 cm   3 cm   5 cm

10 cm

flap

flap

3 cm

flap

8 What have you made?

9 What shape is
each face?

Don't throw your
box away.

The flaps are
for sticking the
box together.

10 Make this net.
Decorate it and fold
it to make a
gift box.

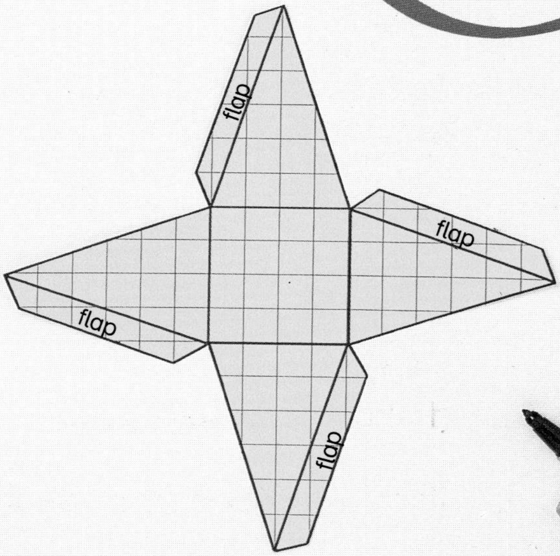

flap

flap

flap

flap

11 What shape is
the box?

12 What shape is its base?

Keep both shapes.
You may need them later.

13 Use a template to draw this net.

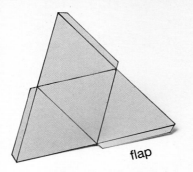

flap

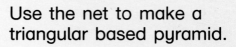

Use the net to make a triangular based pyramid.

14 Why do you think the shape is called this?

Keep your shape.

Let's investigate

What prism shapes can you see in the classroom?
How many can you think of at home?
Record your findings.

B Write the shapes of the faces of each prism.
Use solid shapes to help you.

2 faces are _____
4 faces are _____

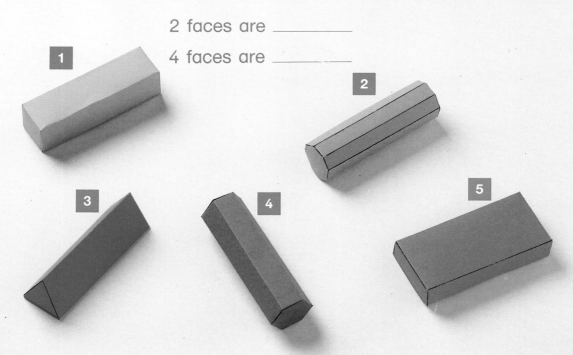

Look at the boxes you made in Section A.

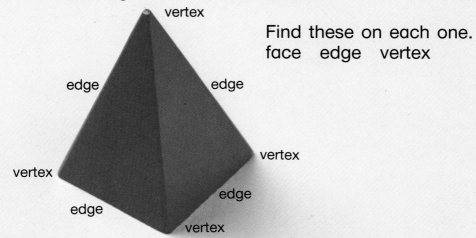

vertex

Find these on each one.
face   edge   vertex

edge   edge

vertex

vertex

edge

edge

vertex

6   Count the number of faces, vertices and edges and complete this table.

Shape	Faces	Vertices	Edges
Rectangular prism			
Square based pyramid			
Triangular based pyramid			
Cube			

7   What do you notice about the numbers?

Let's investigate

Draw round a regular pentagon.

Find a way of making it into a net for a pyramid.

39

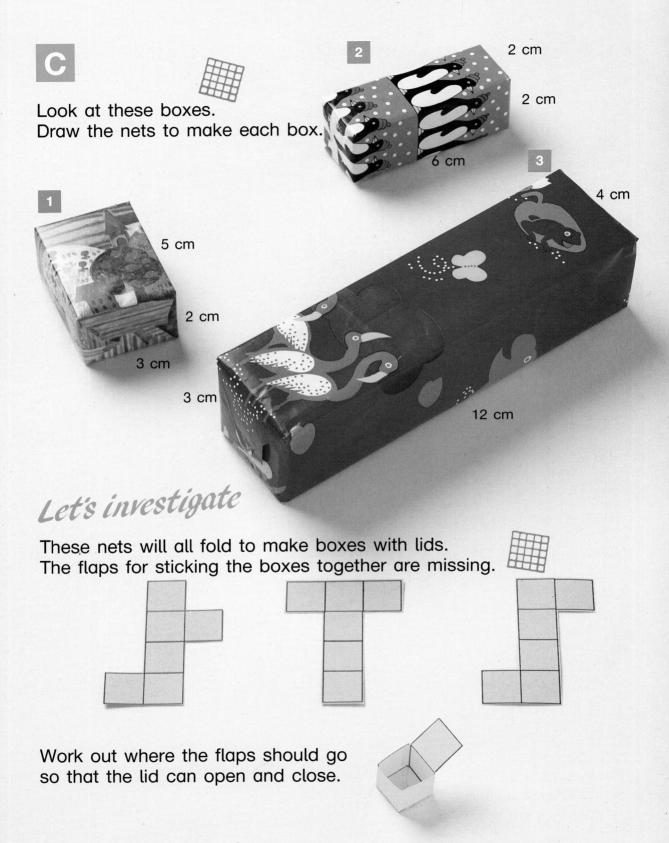

C

Look at these boxes.
Draw the nets to make each box.

2
2 cm
2 cm
6 cm

1
5 cm
2 cm
3 cm

3
4 cm
3 cm
12 cm

Let's investigate

These nets will all fold to make boxes with lids.
The flaps for sticking the boxes together are missing.

Work out where the flaps should go
so that the lid can open and close.

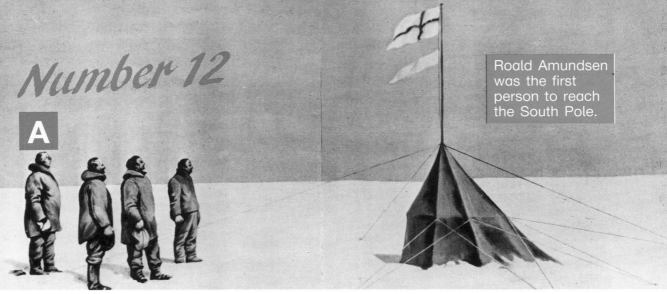

Number 12

A

Roald Amundsen was the first person to reach the South Pole.

Roald Amundsen set off to the South Pole from his base camp on 19 October 1911. He arrived on 14 December 1911.

1 How many days did it take him to reach the Pole?

2 How many weeks was this?

His whole journey there and back took 98 days.

3 How many weeks was he away altogether?

4 Was he quicker or slower on his return journey?

An explorer travelled the following distances.
What was the average distance a day for each?

5 152 km in 4 days   6 112 km in 7 days

7 115 km in 5 days   8 108 km in 4 days

9 112 km in 4 days   10 102 km in 3 days

Let's investigate

Use a calendar.
Choose some dates and ask a friend to work out the number of weeks and days between them.
Write an answer card for each of your questions.

B

Nov 1

⛺ Bluff depot

⛺ One Ton depot

Mar 19 + last camp

Mar 1   ⛺ Mid Barrier depot

QUEEN ALEXANDER RANGE

BEARDMORE GLACIER

Dec 1 S Barrier depot ⛺

⛺ Lower Glacier depot

⛺ Mid Glacier depot

⛺ Upper Glacier depot

Feb 1

⛺ 3 Degree depot
Jan 1

⛺ 1½ Degree depot

⛺ Last depot

Jan 18 1912

Captain Robert Scott set off from his camp to the South Pole on 1 November 1911. On 4 January 1912 he was 320 km from the Pole.

1 How many days had he been travelling?

2 How many weeks and days was this?

If he travelled 23 km each day how far would he have gone after these days?

3 5 days   **4** 8 days   **5** 10 days

Scott reached the South Pole on 18 January 1912.

6 How many weeks and days did his journey take him altogether?

Amundsen's flag was put at the South Pole on 14 December 1911.

7 How many weeks was this before Scott arrived?

Scott's last diary entry was 29 March 1912.

8 How many weeks and days was this after he had reached the pole?

Scott and his friends died on the way back from the South Pole. They were 16 km from a food store.

1912 was a leap year.

Let's investigate

Find some distances between 50 km and 200 km which will each divide exactly by all the numbers 2, 3, 4, 5 and 6.

C

There is an American scientific base at the South Pole today. Many countries have scientific bases in Antarctica. No one country owns Antarctica.

Modern equipment is now used on expeditions to cross the Antarctic.
How far on average would an expedition travel in 1 day if it covered these distances?

1 675 km in 9 days   2 712 km in 8 days

3 904 km in 8 days   4 603 km in 9 days

5 544 km in 8 days   6 801 km in 9 days

Let's investigate

If an expedition travelled 3500 km in 99 days, about how far on average might it travel in 1 day?
Think of a way of doing this without a calculator.
Think of ways of finding the average if the journey took 49 or 69 days.

Data 4

A

At a party, 12 children play Kim's Game. The game is to see how many of the 20 objects you can remember when they are covered up.

The children's scores were grouped together like this.

Number of objects remembered	1–5	6–10	11–15	16–20
Number of children	1	4	5	2

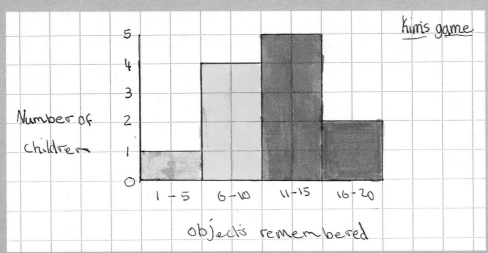

1 The children played again with 25 objects.
Draw a graph for these results.

Objects remembered	1–5	6–10	11–15	16–20	21–25
Number of children	0	1	9	1	1

44

2 Were the results better on the second game?

3 Why do you think this was?

The children play a game of picking up peas with a straw and moving them to another plate.

The top score was 20, the lowest was 1.

4 Put the scores into 5 groups to complete this table.

Scores	1–4	□–□	□–□	□–□	17–20
Children	1	2	5	3	1

5 Draw a graph for the five groups of scores.

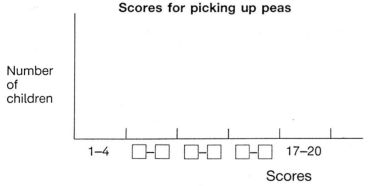

Let's investigate

The top score in a game was 40.
The lowest score was 1.
Find different ways of grouping these scores.

1–□	□–□	□–

A class of 20 children played non-stop cricket.

These were the scores at the end of the game.

Player	1	2	3	4	5	6	7	8	9	10
Score	53	2	41	7	8	29	69	15	35	24
Player	11	12	13	14	15	16	17	18	19	20
Score	42	25	17	21	44	4	70	32	49	36

1 Group the scores and complete this table.

Score group	1–10	☐–☐					61–70
Number of children	4						

2 Use the table to draw a graph.

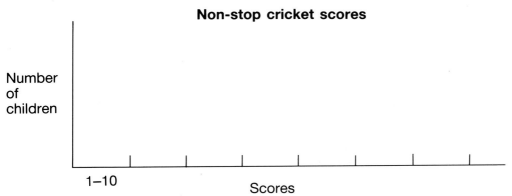

Non-stop cricket scores

Number
of
children

1–10

Scores

46

30 children skip.
They count the number of skips they each do without tripping.
The lowest score is 1, the highest is 60.

3 Show the scores on a graph.
Decide how many children there might be in each group.

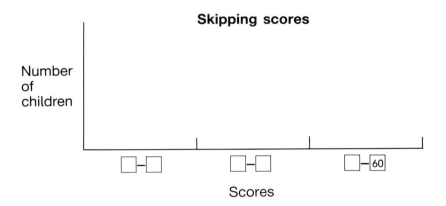

Skipping scores

Number
of
children

Scores

☐—☐ ☐—☐ ☐—60

Let's investigate

Work with some friends.
Think of a game that you might play together in the classroom
or in PE.
You must be able to score points.
Estimate what your scores might be.
Show how you might group the scores for drawing a graph.

C Let's investigate

10 children tried to score goals at netball.
They had 20 shots each and
scored 100 goals between them.

This is a graph of
the goals.

Goals scored

Don't forget the scores add up to 100.

Number of children / Goals

Complete the table to show the scores that each child might have got.

Child	1	2	3	4	5	6	7	8	9	10
Goals										

Do it again using some different numbers.

Area

A What is the area of each advertisement?

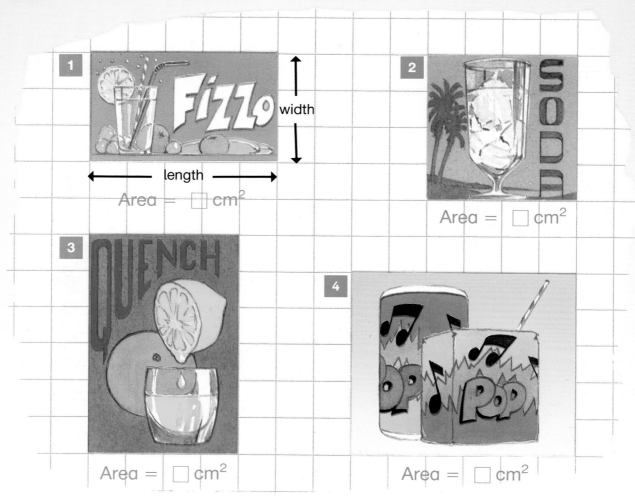

1 width length Area = ☐ cm²

2 Area = ☐ cm²

3 Area = ☐ cm²

4 Area = ☐ cm²

5 Finish this table for the advertisements.

	Length	Width	Area
Fizzo Soda Quench Pop			

The advertisement with the largest area costs the most.

6 Which is the most expensive advertisement?

7 Which is the cheapest?

Write the area of each advertisement.

8 6 cm · SUDS · 3 cm

Area = ☐ cm²

9 5 cm · Washo powder · 4 cm

10 2 cm · CLEAN LIQUID DETERGENT · 5 cm

11 8 cm · BRIGHT WASHES WHITE · 4 cm

12 Finish this table for the advertisements.

	Length	Width	Area
Suds Washo Clean Bright			

Let's investigate

Draw different rectangular advertisements.
Draw a table for their length, width and area.
Explain what you notice about the length, width and area of rectangles.

Look at the page of advertisements.
Measure the length and width of each advertisement.
Make a table which shows the areas and perimeters.

> Perimeter is the distance all round.

1

BOOKS ARE FUN

Come to the book club every Monday lunchtime.

2

RABBITS

Four baby rabbits need a friendly home. Contact the school office.
Remember - a pet is for life.

4

FESTIVAL OF DANCE

next week during assembly. Dances from around the world. Is your class ready?

3

URGENT

Plastic bottles,
egg boxes,
cereal packets,
margarine tubs
and
yogurt pots are all needed by
YOUR
teacher.
Please bring in as many as possible.

5

COMPETITION

*D*esign a poster for your favourite book.
Entries must be handed to your teacher by Friday.
1st prize - £10 book token.

6 ☞ SWOPS

ROBOT ROBOT ROBOT

Good condition.
Will swop for computer games.
Contact Class 4.

7

TEACHERS -v- CHILDREN

NETBALL MATCH.

Don't miss it!

8 **CHESS CLUB**

Forget the rest,
Chess is the best!

9

LOST!!

A bright red lunchbox.
Please return to Class 2.

10   What is the perimeter of the advertisement page?

Find the areas and perimeters of these photographs.

15 Finish this table for the photographs.

Length	Width	Area	Perimeter
1 cm			
2 cm			
3 cm			
4 cm			
☐ cm		25 cm²	
☐ cm			24 cm

16 A square photograph has a perimeter of 28 cm.
What is its area?

17 A square photograph has an area of 64 cm².
What is its perimeter?

18 Use two photographs from a magazine.
Cut each one into a rectangle with an area of 48 cm².
The rectangles must be different shapes.

19 Draw two rectangles, each one 8 cm by 12 cm.

20 Cut one of the rectangles to make one square and one smaller rectangle.
Stick them in your book.
Write the area of each shape.

21 Cut the other rectangle to make two squares and one rectangle.
Stick them in your book.
Write their areas.

Let's investigate

Draw a plan for an advertisement 6 cm by 4 cm.

Draw squares or rectangles to fill the plan
exactly. Each one must have an area of 4 cm².
Find different ways to do it.

C

1. Cut out four different advertisements
from a newspaper. Stick them in
your book and work out their areas.

Let's investigate

Draw some squares and rectangles which have the same perimeters
as each other. Find whether the square or the rectangle has the
larger area when the perimeter is the same.

Data 5

A

Jan went from
Edinburgh to Oxford.
This is a graph of
part of her motorway
journey.

Graph of motorway journey

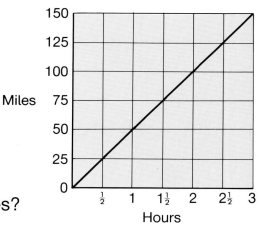

1 How far had she gone after 1 hour?

2 How far had she gone after 90 minutes?

3 How long did it take her to travel 100 miles?

4 How far did she travel in the first $2\frac{1}{2}$ hours?

Jan's car broke down after 3 hours.
This table is a record of her journey.

Time in hours	0	1	2	3	4	5
Miles	0	50	100	150	150	200

How far had she travelled after these hours?

5 3 hours   **6** 4 hours   **7** 5 hours?

8 How long did she stop for?

9 How far did she travel during the last hour of her journey?

10 Use the table to draw a graph of her journey.

Let's investigate

Susan took 7 hours for the same journey.
She travelled at different speeds and made two stops.
Find different ways to complete the table.

Time in hours	0	1	2	3	4	5	6	7
Miles	0							200

Alexander Graham Bell invented the telephone in 1876.
The phone card was first used in 1986.

At lunchtime Jan stopped to make a telephone call.
She used her phonecard.

1 Copy and finish the table.

Units on phonecard	0	1	2	3	4	5	6	7	8	9	10
Cost in pence	0	10	20	30							

2 How many units will 70p buy?

3 Jan used 9 units. How much did this cost?

4 Use the table to draw a line graph for the cost of telephone units.

How far did she travel between these times?

Graph of Jan's journey after lunch

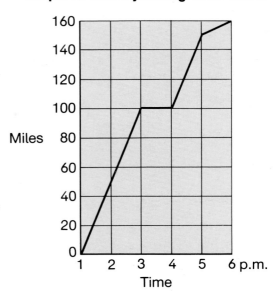

5 | 1 p.m. and 3 p.m.

6 | 1 p.m. and 4 p.m.

7 | 4 p.m. and 5 p.m.

8 | 5 p.m. and 6 p.m.

9 | Copy and finish the table.

Time	1 p.m.	2 p.m.	3 p.m.	4 p.m.	5 p.m.	6 p.m.
Miles	0					

Let's investigate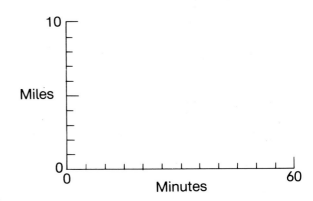

Why do you think Jan only travelled 10 miles in the last 60 minutes? Show this part of her journey on a graph. Explain why she might have been so slow.

57

C

Jan made a diary of her journey.

	Time	Distance travelled
left Edinburgh	7 a.m.	0 miles
	8 a.m.	50 miles
	9 a.m.	100 miles
broke down	10 a.m.	150 miles
set off	11 a.m.	150 miles
lunch and phone	12 noon	200 miles
set off again	1 p.m.	200 miles
	2 p.m.	250 miles
drink and rest	3 p.m.	300 miles
set off again	4 p.m.	300 miles
	5 p.m.	350 miles
arrived at Oxford	6 p.m.	360 miles

1 Draw a line graph of Jan's journey.

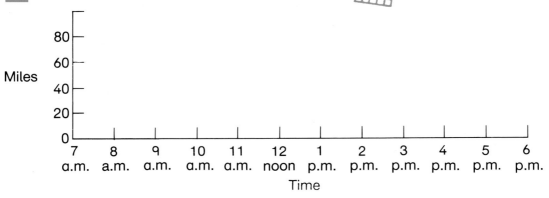

2 How far was her journey?   **3** How long did it take?

4 Did she travel further before lunch or after?

Let's investigate

Nadim and Jenny each make the same 200 mile car journey.
They set off at the same time and arrive together.
Jenny makes one stop, Nadim makes two.
Show both journeys on the same graph.

Weight 2

A

Dinosaurs, or 'terrible lizards' lived millions of years before there were any people.

Estimated dinosaur weights	
Allosaurus	2000 kg
Iguanodon	4500 kg
Stegosaurus	1800 kg
Torvosaurus	5400 kg

1000 kg = 1 tonne
or 1·000 tonne

Copy this chart and fill it in.

Allosaurus	2000 kg	2·000 tonnes
1 Iguanodon		
2 Stegosaurus		
3 Torvosaurus		

Look at these pairs of dinosaurs.
Which of each pair weighs more?

4 Allosaurus
Iguanodon

5 Iguanodon
Torvosaurus

6 Stegosaurus
Torvosaurus

7 Allosaurus
Stegosaurus

8 Torvosaurus
Allosaurus

9 Stegosaurus
Iguanodon

An allosaurus

Estimated dinosaur weights	
Allosaurus	2000 kg
Tyrannosaurus	6400 kg
Stegosaurus	1800 kg
Torvosaurus	5400 kg

1 tonne is 1000 kg.

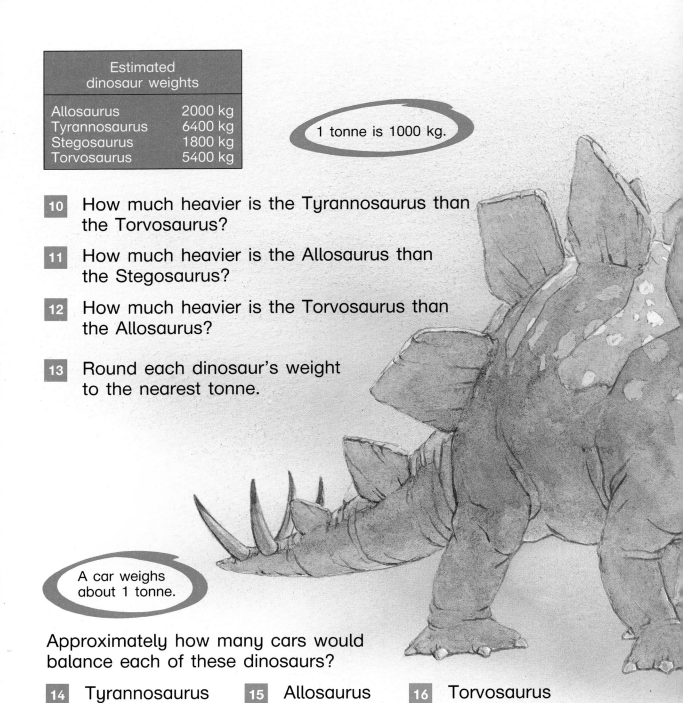

10 How much heavier is the Tyrannosaurus than the Torvosaurus?

11 How much heavier is the Allosaurus than the Stegosaurus?

12 How much heavier is the Torvosaurus than the Allosaurus?

13 Round each dinosaur's weight to the nearest tonne.

A car weighs about 1 tonne.

Approximately how many cars would balance each of these dinosaurs?

14 Tyrannosaurus   **15** Allosaurus   **16** Torvosaurus

Let's investigate

Make a list of things that will weigh more than a tonne.

B

Estimated dinosaur weights	
Megalosaurus	0·900 tonnes
Tyrannosaurus	6·400 tonnes
Triceratops	5·400 tonnes
Iguanodon	4·500 tonnes

1 Change the dinosaur weights into kg.

Write them in order.
Start with the lightest.

Find the difference, in kg, between the weights of these dinosaurs.

2 Tyrannosaurus
Iguanodon

3 Iguanodon
Megalosaurus

4 Megalosaurus
Tyrannosaurus

5 Triceratops
Iguanodon

The Stegosaurus had two pairs of sharp spikes at the end of its tail. They were a very dangerous weapon.

A Stegosaurus

6 Find out how many times heavier the Triceratops was than the Megalosaurus. Explain how you did it.

7 Find out how many Megalosaurus dinosaurs would have balanced one Iguanodon.

8 Two of the dinosaurs balance one of the others.
Which are they?

9 Round the weight of each dinosaur to the nearest tonne.
Show these weights on a graph.

Estimated dinosaur weights	
Diplodocus	10·600 tonnes
Triceratops	5·400 tonnes
Tyrannosaurus	6·400 tonnes
Megalosaurus	0·900 tonnes

Aeroplanes are weighed in tonnes.
When a Boeing 757 begins to taxi down the runway it can weigh up to 100 tonnes.

Approximately how many of each dinosaur would balance the Boeing 757?

10 Megalosaurus   **11** Diplodocus

12 Tyrannosaurus   **13** Triceratops

Let's investigate

Think of ways to work out approximately how many children of your age would together weigh 1 tonne.

C

The remains of the Ultrasaurus (ultra lizard) were discovered in Colorado in the USA in 1979.

Scientists estimate the basic weight of the dinosaurs.
At their fattest they may have weighed about a third more than their basic weight.
Find the approximate fattest weight for these big dinosaurs.

		Basic weight	Fattest weight
1	Ultrasaurus	about 48 tonnes	about ☐ tonnes
2	Brachiosaurus	about 36 tonnes	about ☐ tonnes
3	Titanosaurus	about 54 tonnes	about ☐ tonnes

4   Show the basic weights on a bar chart.

5   Show the fattest weights on the same chart.
    Use a different colour.

basic weight
fattest weight

Let's investigate

Use reference books.
Compare the weights of some of the largest animals in the world today with any of the dinosaurs.
Show your findings in an interesting way.

A 5-day holidays in Britain

Travel agents book holidays for people. They use charts like these to help people plan where to stay and work out how much it will cost.

Hotel	Code
Royal	A
Bay View	B
Anchor	C
Fisherman	D
West	E
Marina	F
Majestic	G

This chart shows how much it costs one person to stay for 5 days at the hotels.

Departure day and date		A £	B £	C £	D £	E £	F £	G £
Sunday	20 March	78	78	78	80	78	80	78
Thursday	24 March	78	78	78	80	78	80	78
Monday	28 March	82	82	82	84	82	84	82
Friday	1 April	90	90	90	92	90	92	90
Tuesday	5 April	87	87	87	89	87	89	87
Saturday	9 April	82	82	82	84	82	84	82
Wednesday	13 April	82	82	82	84	82	84	82

1 Copy and finish this chart.

Date	Cost	Hotel
24 March		Fisherman
5 April		Majestic
28 March		Royal
1 April		Anchor

Find the cost of these 5-day holidays for two people.

2 The Bay View from 24 March

3 The Marina from 9 April

4 The Fisherman from 20 March

5 The Anchor from 1 April

Holidays in Germany

Cost for one person from London		By rail			By air		
Number of nights		3	7	10	3	7	10
Hotel		£	£	£	£	£	£
Kramer	BB	151	200	235	171	213	249
Alpenrose	BB	151	200	235	171	213	249
Glocke	BB	182	269	334	197	281	348
Danube	BB	183	275	344	198	288	358
Seegarten	BB	215	345	442	225	357	456

BB: Bed and breakfast

Find the costs of these holidays.

	Hotel	Nights	Travel
6	Glocke	7	Air
7	Alpenrose	3	Rail
8	Danube	10	Air
9	Kramer	7	Rail

How did these holiday makers travel?

	Hotel	Cost
10	Alpenrose	£213
11	Seegarten	£357
12	Danube	£183
13	Kramer	£249

How much will these holidays at the hotel Kramer cost for 2 people?

14 7 nights by rail

15 7 nights by air

16 What is the difference in the cost of the two holidays?

Let's investigate

Use the chart.
Find some holidays in Germany that cost less than £500 for two people.

B Holidays to Brussels, Luxembourg or Bruges

By air from London to Brussels
By air from London to Luxembourg
By coach and hovercraft from London to Brussels
By train and ferry from London to Bruges

Reductions for children under 12

£5 per child
£7 per child
£8 per child
£18 per child

Hotels	1* £	2* £	3* £	4* £
3 nights	151	176	206	213
	—	166	192	214
	99	125	155	162
	98	114	135	156
5 nights	185	227	280	289
	—	209	255	288
	133	176	229	238
	139	166	202	236
7 nights	219	278	354	365
	—	251	317	362
	167	227	303	313
	174	212	264	310

Find the costs of these holidays for one adult and a child.

	Place	Nights	Hotel	Cost per person	Cost per child	Total
1	Luxembourg	3	3*	£ ☐	£ ☐	£ ☐
2	Brussels (air)	7	2*	£ ☐	£ ☐	£ ☐
3	Bruges	5	4*	£ ☐	£ ☐	£ ☐
4	Brussels (coach)	5	1*	£ ☐	£ ☐	£ ☐

Find the costs of these holidays for two adults.

	Place	Nights	Hotel	Cost
5	Brussels (air)	5	2*	£ ☐
6	Bruges	3	4*	£ ☐
7	Brussels (coach)	7	3*	£ ☐
8	Luxembourg	5	2*	£ ☐

9 Find the difference between the cheapest and the most expensive holiday in the chart.

10 Find the difference between the cheapest and most expensive holiday in a 4* hotel.

Find the costs of these holidays.

---

11 | Travel: London to Brussels

Hotel   4*   Number of adults   2
Number of nights   3   Number of children
By air
By coach and hovercraft ✓
By train and ship

---

12 | Travel: London to Luxembourg

Hotel   2*   Number of adults   3
Number of nights   7   Number of children
By air ✓
By coach and hovercraft
By train and ship

---

13 | Travel: London to Bruges

Hotel   1*   Number of adults   1
Number of nights   3   Number of children   1
By air
By coach and hovercraft
By train and ship ✓

Let's investigate

Choose a holiday from the chart.
Make a form and fill it in for you and your family.
What is the total cost?

Holidays in Barbados

Find the costs of these holidays.

1 3 adults at the Treasure Beach for 7 days departing on Wednesday 5 July.

2 2 adults at the Royal Pavilion for 14 days departing on Saturday 8 April.

Departures on or between	01 Dec- 06 Dec 89		07 Dec- 31 Dec 89		01 Jan- 31 Mar 90		01 Apr- 30 Apr		01 May- 31 May		01 Jun- 30 Jun		01 Jul- 31 Aug		01 Sep- 24 Oct		25 Oct- 30 Nov	
Hotel	7	14	7	14	7	14	7	14	7	14	7	14	7	14	7	14	7	14
Treasure Beach	885	1260	1172	1650	1009	1483	633	873	619	843	611	833	715	940	627	857	643	887
Royal Pavilion	1009	1353	1535	2390	1393	2250	945	1470	779	1165	772	1156	878	1266	791	1191	972	1544
Coral Reef Club	1136	1694	1462	2208	1245	1950	885	1236	798	1102	776	1085	882	1195	795	1116	898	1262
Kings Beach	766	939	983	1260	766	996	567	740	564	737	560	731	663	836	574	749	575	751

3 Which is the most expensive time to visit Barbados?

4 Which is the cheapest time to visit Barbados?

Let's investigate

Use some travel brochures for holidays in exotic places.
Plan a very expensive holiday for yourself and a friend.
Show how you work out the cost.

Probability 2

A

1 How many ways can you throw a total score of 4 using two dice?

1st dice   1st dice   1st dice

2nd dice   2nd dice   2nd dice

How many ways are there of throwing these totals using two dice each time?
Write all the ways in a table like this.

2 Total of 5

1st dice	2nd dice	Total
2	3	5

3 Total of 7

4 Total of 10

69

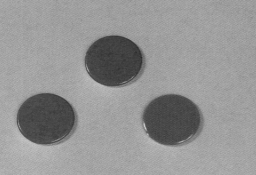

5 How many different ways can you arrange the colours on the 'start'?
Draw your answers like this.

6 Do the same with these counters.

7 Are there more ways with three colours?

Let's investigate

You have two pots with three numbered counters in each.
You take one counter from each pot
and add their scores.
You put the counters back and do
the same again.

Write all the possible scores you
could make.

70

B

1. Make a chart like this.

2. Show on the chart the different coloured games kits you could make from these tops and shorts.

Colour of shorts	Colour of top

3. How many different kits could you make?

4. How many different kits would there be if there were just two pairs of shorts?

5. How many different kits would there be if there was just one pair of shorts?

6. How many kits do you think there would be if there were 4 pairs of shorts?

Four children are playing in a chess tournament.
Each one has to play a game with all the others.

7 Draw a chart or diagram to show how many games are played by the 4 children altogether.

8 Draw a chart or diagram to show the number of games they would play altogether if Kevin joined them.

Let's investigate

Work out chess matches for different groups of children in your class so that each child plays everyone else in the group.

Give the names of the players and make charts to show the matches.

Write about any number patterns you see.

C

Suna enjoys playing table tennis.
He made a pattern to work out what might happen in his next 3 games.

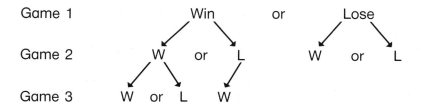

Game 1   Win   or   Lose

Game 2   W   or   L   W   or   L

Game 3   W   or   L   W

1   Finish the pattern for Suna.

2   Use the pattern to find how many different ways he could win two out of the three games.
    Answer like this:

    First way   W → W → L

Let's investigate

The school skittleball team plays 3 games.
Try to work out all the possible results for the 3 games.

Remember, a team can win, lose or draw in skittleball.

Shape 4

A

1 Use a square.
Make a template like this.

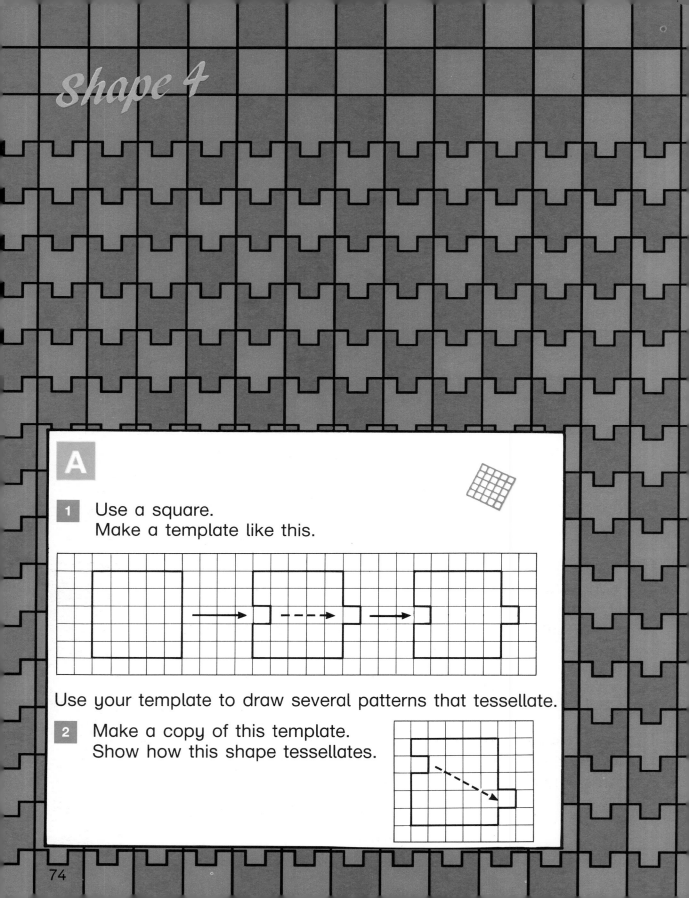

Use your template to draw several patterns that tessellate.

2 Make a copy of this template.
Show how this shape tessellates.

3 Some designs are made from a template like this.

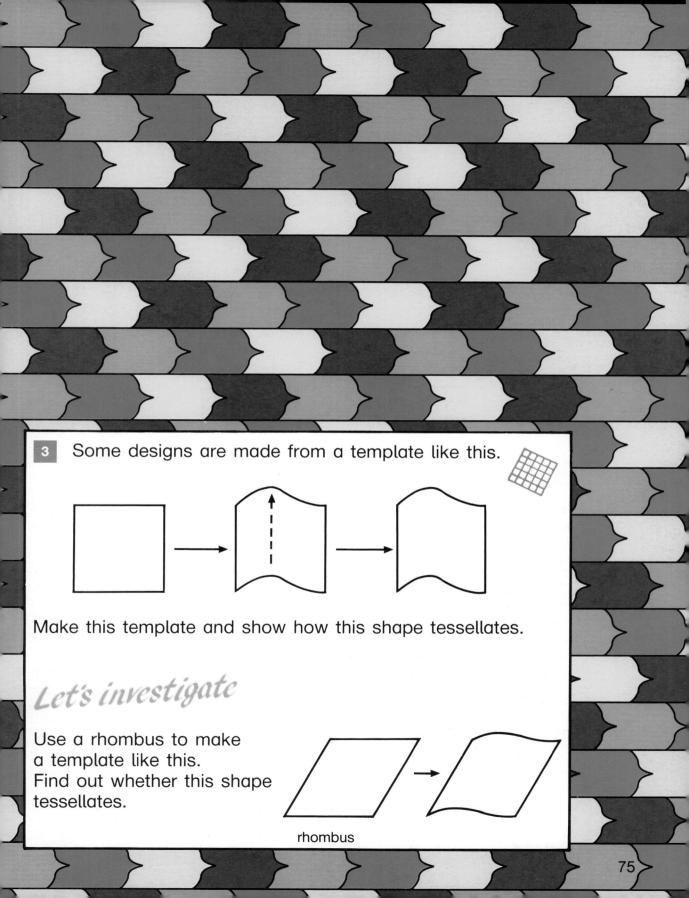

Make this template and show how this shape tessellates.

Let's investigate

Use a rhombus to make
a template like this.
Find out whether this shape
tessellates.

rhombus

B

1. Use a square and make a template like this.

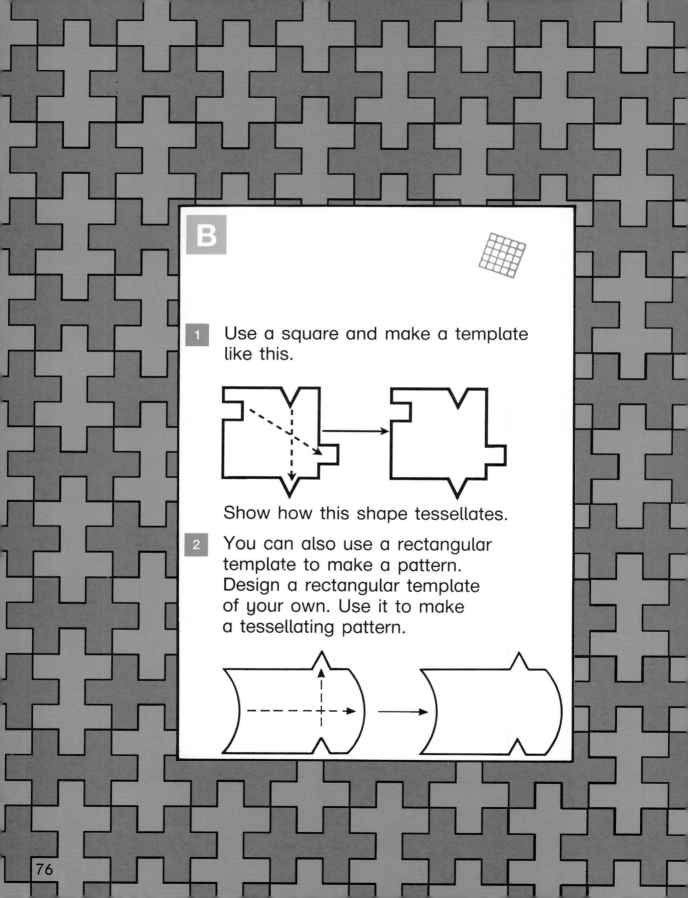

Show how this shape tessellates.

2. You can also use a rectangular template to make a pattern. Design a rectangular template of your own. Use it to make a tessellating pattern.

Let's investigate

Use two parallelograms and put them together like this.

Draw round your shape to make a template. Can you make your new shape tessellate?

Try to make different tessellating patterns with other shapes made from two parallelograms.

C

1 Use two equal squares and cut them like this.

Use the template to make a design.

Let's investigate

Use two equal parallelograms
to make this shape.
Will it tessellate?

Design another shape
that will tessellate, using
two equal parallelograms.

Number 13

A

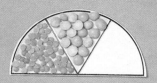

Diwali is the Hindu Festival of Light. To celebrate it, people often make designs on their doorsteps with coloured rice, peas and lentils.

These patterns are not finished.
Write the fraction sums for the coloured parts
of the seed patterns.

1

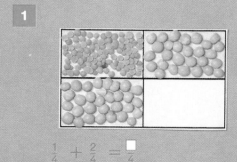

$\frac{1}{4} + \frac{2}{4} = \frac{\square}{4}$

What fraction is not finished?

2

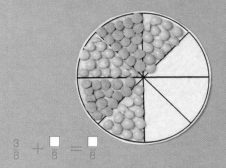

$\frac{3}{8} + \frac{\square}{8} = \frac{\square}{8}$

What fraction is not finished?

3

$\frac{\square}{5} + \frac{2}{5} = \frac{\square}{5}$

What fraction is not finished?

4

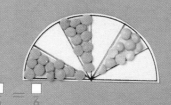

$\frac{2}{6} + \frac{\square}{6} = \frac{\square}{6}$

What fraction is not finished?

5 Draw and colour.

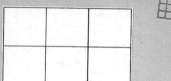

Colour $\frac{1}{6}$ yellow.
Colour $\frac{4}{6}$ green.

$\frac{1}{6} + \frac{4}{6} = \frac{\square}{6}$

6 Draw and colour.

Colour $\frac{2}{5}$ red.
Colour $\frac{1}{5}$ black.

$\frac{\square}{5} + \frac{\square}{5} = \frac{\square}{\square}$

7

$\frac{\square}{4} + \frac{\square}{4} + \frac{\square}{4} + \frac{\square}{4} = \frac{4}{4}$

$= 1$ whole shape

8

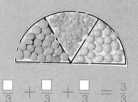

$\frac{\square}{3} + \frac{\square}{3} + \frac{\square}{3} = \frac{3}{3}$

$= 1$ whole shape

1 whole shape $+ \frac{1}{4} = 1\frac{1}{4}$

9

$1 + \frac{\square}{2} = \square$

Let's investigate

The fraction sentence for the coloured parts in this shape is
$\frac{2}{8} + \frac{3}{8} = \frac{5}{8}$.

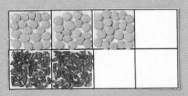

Colour this shape in different ways.
Write a fraction sentence for each one.

B Write the fraction sums for the coloured parts of the patterns.

1 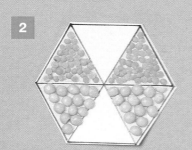 $\frac{3}{5} + \frac{1}{5} = \square$

2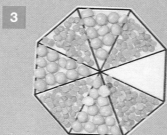

3

4

5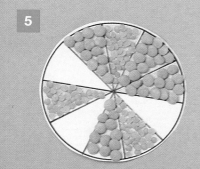

6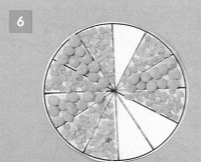

7 $\frac{2}{10} + \frac{3}{10} + \frac{4}{10} = \square$

8 $\frac{3}{8} + \frac{1}{8} + \frac{2}{8} = \square$

9 $\frac{4}{12} + \frac{2}{12} + \frac{3}{12} = \square$

10 $\frac{5}{12} + \frac{2}{12} + \frac{4}{12} = \square$

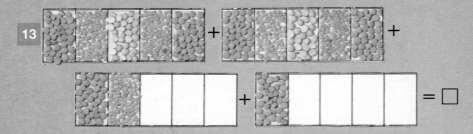

$$\boxed{\times} + \boxed{\times} + \boxed{\times} = 2\tfrac{1}{2}$$

1 whole   1 whole $\frac{1}{2}$

Write the fractions for the coloured parts of these shapes.

11   ⊠ + ⊠ + ⊠ = ☐

12   ▦ + ▦ + ▦ = ☐

13   ▦ + ▦ +

▦ + ▦ = ☐

Let's investigate

Look at the coloured parts of these shapes.

Add any three of them each time.
What different fractions can you make?

C $\frac{5}{4} = \frac{4}{4} + \frac{1}{4} = 1\tfrac{1}{4}$

Show these fractions in the same way.

1   $\frac{6}{4}$ 2 $\frac{9}{8}$

3   $\frac{11}{8}$ 4 $\frac{10}{6}$

Let's investigate

$\frac{\square}{\square} = 1\frac{\square}{\square}$ Find as many numbers as you can to fit this fraction sentence.

82

Angles 2

A

Lucy is giving instructions
for Joe to make a square.

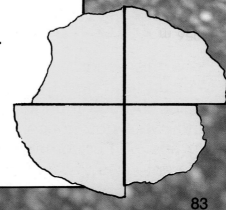

> Forward 10 paces
> Right 90°
> Forward 10 paces
> Right 90°
> Forward 10 paces
> Right 90°
> Forward 10 paces
> Right 90°

1. Draw these instructions on squared paper
   making each pace 1 cm.

2. Measure the angles of your square and add them.
   $\square° + \square° + \square° + \square° = \square°$

3. Draw a larger square. Add all the angles.
   What do you find?

4. Cut out your square.
   Tear off the corners and put
   them together like this.
   How many degrees do the
   angles of the square add up to?

5 Read the instructions to make this rectangle. Draw the rectangle on squared paper making each pace 1 cm.

6 How many right angles does the rectangle have?

Forward 7 paces
Right 90°
Forward 10 paces
Right 90°
Forward 7 paces
Right 90°
Forward 10 paces
Right 90°

7 Draw in the diagonal line on your rectangle. What shapes have you made?

8 Colour one triangle blue and one red. Measure the angles of the red triangle and add them together.

$\Box° + \Box° + \Box° = \Box°$

9 Measure and add the angles of the blue triangle.

10 What do the angles of each triangle add up to?

Let's investigate

Draw this square. Measure and add the angles of each triangle. Write what you notice. Try this with squares of different sizes.

B Measure these angles.

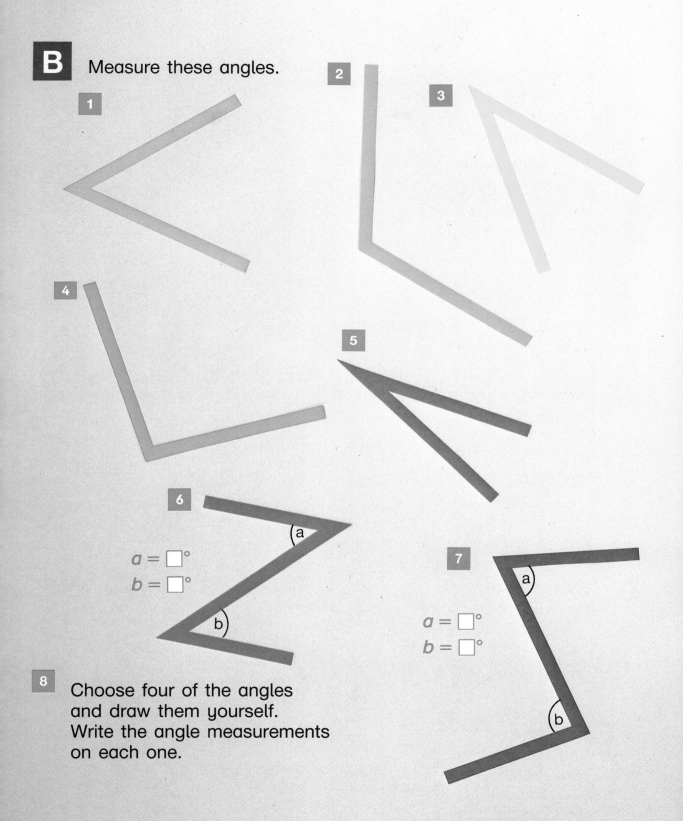

1

2

3

4

5

6

$a = \square°$
$b = \square°$

(a

b)

7

$a = \square°$
$b = \square°$

a)

b

8 Choose four of the angles and draw them yourself. Write the angle measurements on each one.

Measure the angles of these triangles and add them.

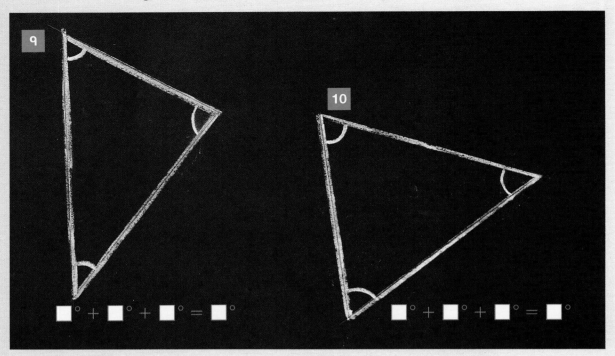

$\square° + \square° + \square° = \square°$

$\square° + \square° + \square° = \square°$

11 What do the angles of each triangle add up to?

12 Draw your own triangle
on a piece of paper.
Cut it out.

Tear off the angles and
put them together like this.

What do the angles add up to?

Let's investigate

Draw and cut out different triangles. Tear off the angles from
each and put them together.
Explain what you notice.

C

Find the missing angles of these triangles without measuring.

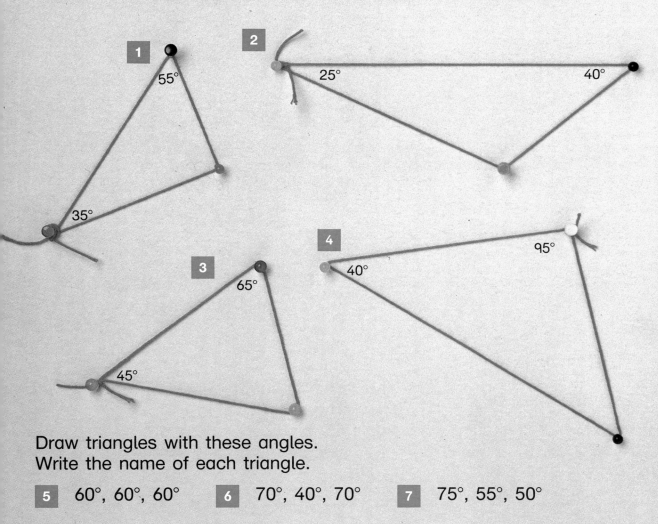

Draw triangles with these angles.
Write the name of each triangle.

5 60°, 60°, 60°   **6** 70°, 40°, 70°   **7** 75°, 55°, 50°

Let's investigate

Draw different triangles.
Each one must have at least one angle of 60°.

Which different types of triangle can you draw?
Are there any types of triangle you cannot draw?

Time 3

A shuttle service flies every day from Manchester to London.

Depart Manchester	Arrive London
06:45	07:40
07:45	
08:45	
09:45	
10:45	
11:45	
12:45	
13:45	
14:45	
15:45	
16:45	
17:45	
18:45	
19:45	20:40

1 This is the shuttle timetable for weekdays. The flight takes 55 minutes.

Copy the timetable and put in the arrival times.

2 How often does the shuttle leave Manchester?

3 What is the earliest flight?

4 What is the last flight?

5 What time does the 15:45 flight arrive in London?

6 What time did the 12:40 arrival take off from Manchester?

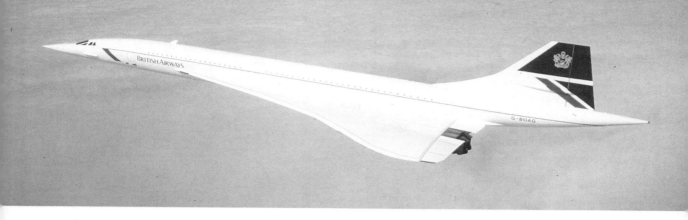

Destination	Departure times
San Francisco	10:00
St Louis	11:00
Washington	11:45
Nice	12:40
Singapore	14:00
Paris	16:30
Johannesburg	18:00
Tokyo	19:00
Sydney	19:45
Rio de Janeiro	22:25

Some people use the shuttle to fly to London to catch flights to other parts of the world.

7 When you arrive in London you need to allow two hours before your next flight. Complete the timetable chart.

Depart Manchester	Arrive London	Allow 2 hours	Next flight
10:45	11:40	13:40	Singapore 14:00
07:45			
09:45			
15:45			
16:45			

8 How long would you wait in London to catch the plane to Sydney if you left Manchester on the 16:45 shuttle?

Let's investigate

Plan some flights from Manchester that give at least 3 hours before take-off on another flight from London. Show the times of the flights.

B   Here is a train timetable from Weston-super-Mare to London.

Mondays to Fridays	IC	IC	IC	IC	IC ✕	IC	IC	IC P	IC	IC ✕
Weston-super-Mare	0838	——	0940	——	1120	——	1202	1224	1255	——
Brisol Temple Meads	0920	——	1020	——	1140	——	1240	1245	1340	——
Bristol Parkway	——	1011	——	1102	——	1202	——	1302	——	1402
Bath Spa	0934	——	1034	——	1152	——	1252	——	1352	——
Chippenham	0945	——	1045	——	1203	——	1303	——	1403	——
Swindon	1000	1038	1100	1129	1220	1229	1318	1329	1418	1429
Didcot Parkway	1017	——	1117	——	1235	——	1335	——	1435	——
Reading ✈	1031	1104	1131	1155	1249	1255	1349	1356	1449	1455
Slough	1106	——	1146	1240	——	1310	1404	1440	1504	1540
London Paddington	1102	1133	1204	1224	1318	1328	1422	1425	1522	1525

IC   **InterCity train** with catering.
P   **InterCity Pullman train.**
✕   **Restaurant.**

1 What time is the train from Bristol Parkway which gets into London before noon?

2 Which train from Weston-super-Mare arrives in London at 3:22 p.m.?

3 Which train from Bristol Parkway gets into London at 2:25 p.m.?

4 Which train leaves Swindon after 2 p.m. and has a restaurant car?

5 Which trains leave Bristol Temple Meads before 12:30?

6 Which train from Bath Spa has a restaurant car?

Let's investigate

Plan a timetable for an evening train journey from Acton to Espley, stopping at Basil, Canwell and Dryden.
The whole journey takes 1 hour 10 minutes.
Use 24 hour clock times.

C Travellers through London often have to change stations.
These are timetables for two London stations.

> ### Arrival times at Paddington from Weston-super-Mare.
> 12:04   13:18   14:22   15:22   16:18

**Departure times
from Euston Station**

Mondays to Fridays

London Euston	1330	1430	1450	1500	1530	1600	1620	1630	—	1705
Kensington Olympia	—	—	—	—	—	—	—	—	1436	—
Watford Junction (dep)	1346	1410	—	—	1510	1616	1636	1646	—	—
Milton Keynes Central	—	1507	1526	1536	1606	—	—	—	—	1633
Rugby	—	—	1556	—	—	—	—	—	—	1805
Nuneaton	1444	—	—	1614	—	—	—	—	—	1818
Tamworth	—	—	1617	—	—	—	—	—	—	—
Stafford	1515	—	1639	—	1707	—	1755	—	—	1847
Crewe	1542	1634	1708	—	—	1754	—	1825	1855	1915
Chester	—	1721	1751	—	—	1835	—	—	—	1951
Holyhead	—	—	1954	—	—	—	—	—	—	2143
Runcorn	—	—	1731	—	—	—	1833	—	—	—
Liverpool Lime Street	—	—	1752	—	—	—	1854	—	—	—

Use the two timetables to copy and complete this chart of
journeys. Allow 1 hour to travel from Paddington to Euston.

Travel from	Arrive at Paddington	Time to get to Euston	Leave Euston	Arrive at
Weston-super-Mare	12:04	Allow 1 hour	13:30	Stafford at 15:15
1 Weston-super-Mare		Allow 1 hour		Milton Keynes at 15:07
2 Weston-super-Mare		Allow 1 hour		Holyhead at 21:43
3 Weston-super-Mare		Allow 1 hour		Crewe at 17:54

Let's investigate

Use train timetables.
Plan a long train journey.
Try to include changing trains in the journey.
Write 24 hour clock times.

Length 2

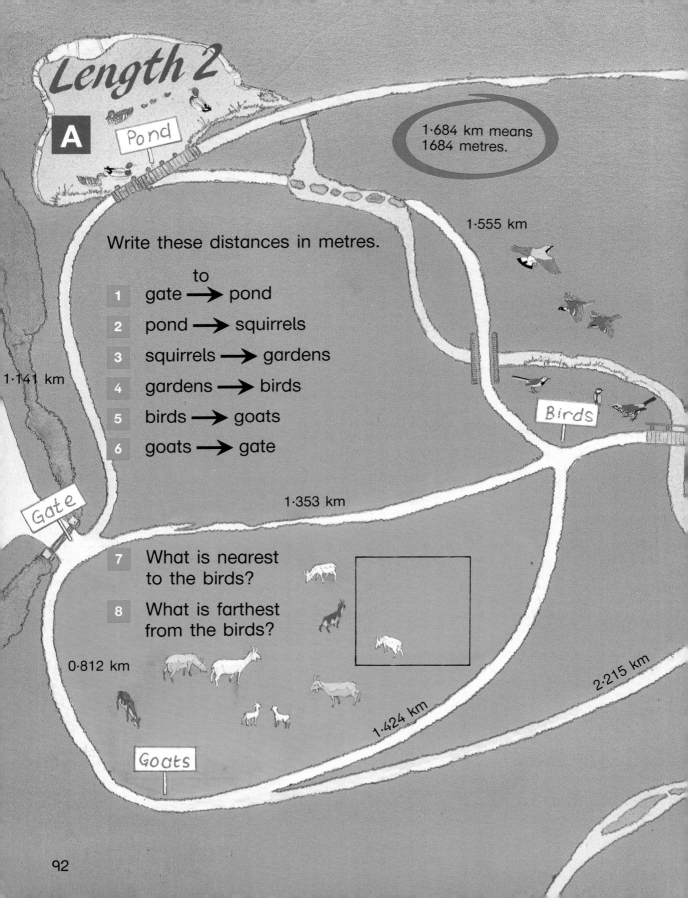

A

Pond

1·684 km means
1684 metres.

1·555 km

Write these distances in metres.

         to

1. gate → pond
2. pond → squirrels
3. squirrels → gardens
4. gardens → birds
5. birds → goats
6. goats → gate

1·141 km

Birds

1·353 km

7. What is nearest to the birds?

8. What is farthest from the birds?

0·812 km

Goats

1·424 km

2·215 km

00 km

Squirrels

Find the shortest distance between these places.

9 gate and gardens **10** goats and pond

11 pond and gardens

12 Find these distances.
goats → gardens
goats → birds → gardens
What is the difference between the two distances?

1·344 km

Gardens

1·024 km

40 m

20 m

30 m

70 m

13 What is the perimeter of the gardens in metres?

14 What is the perimeter in km?

15 The goat pen is square.
It has the same perimeter as the gardens.
What is the length of each side of the pen?

Let's investigate

Draw the plan of a square goat pen with a perimeter of 60 m. Write on the measurements.
Draw some different shaped pens with the same perimeter.
Write on the measurements.

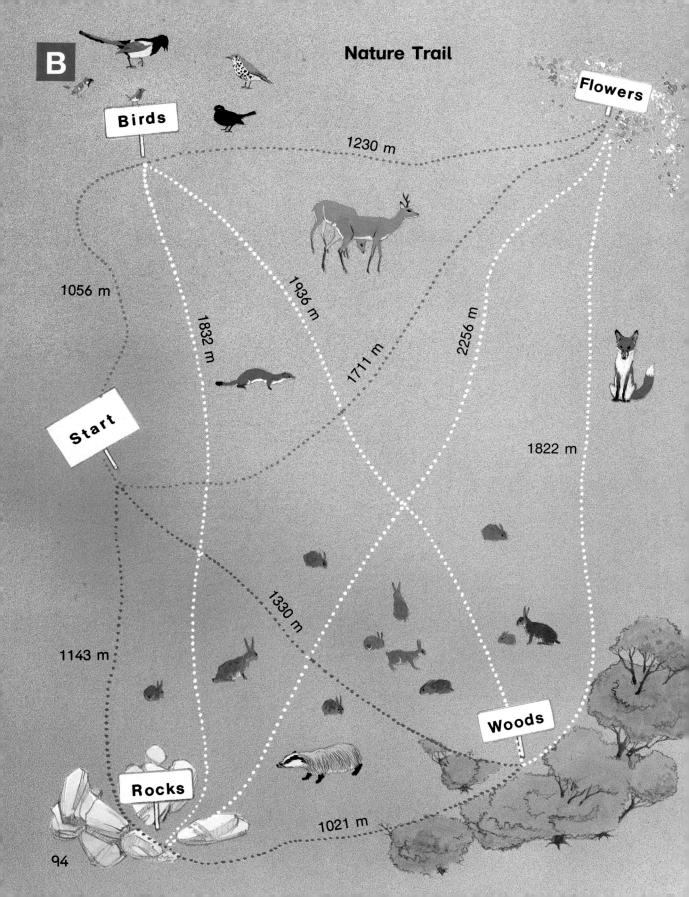

Nature Trail

B

Flowers

Birds

1230 m

1056 m

1936 m

1832 m

1711 m

2256 m

Start

1822 m

1330 m

1143 m

Woods

Rocks

1021 m

94

Write these distances in kilometres.

1 start → birds
2 birds → flowers
3 flowers → woods
4 woods → rocks
5 rocks → start
6 start → flowers

1274 m is 1·274 km.

Find these distances in kilometres.

7 start → birds → flowers
8 flowers → woods → rocks
9 birds → rocks → woods
10 start → rocks → flowers

11 Find the distance round the red trail in km.

12 Find the distance round the blue trail in km.

The straight line distance from the birds to the woods is 1900 m.
The path is 1936 m.

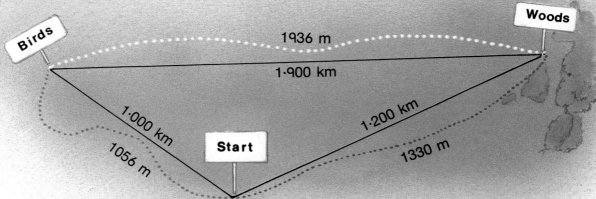

What is the difference between the distance by path and the straight line distances between these places?

13 birds and woods
14 start and birds
15 start and woods

Let's investigate

Visit 3 or more places around the nature trail.
The total distance must be less than 5 km.
Say where you start and finish each time.

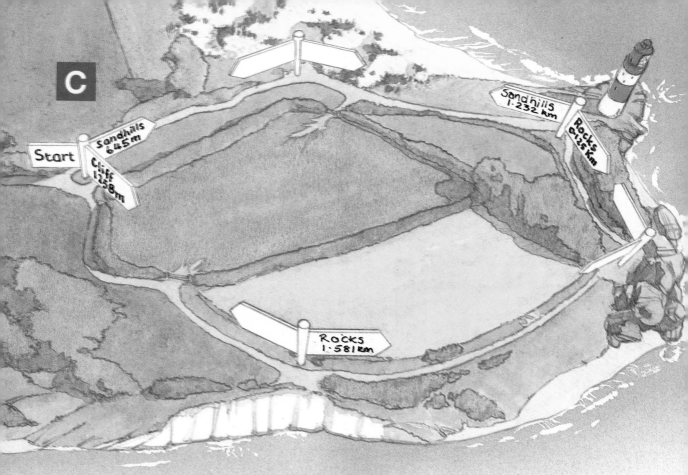

C

Start

sandhills
645 m

Cliff
1·258 m

Sandhills
1·232 km

Rocks
0·125 km

Rocks
1·581 km

Write these distances in metres.

1. sandhills → lighthouse   2. cliff → start

3. rocks → cliff   4. rocks → lighthouse

5. What is the shortest distance from the start to the lighthouse?

6. What is the total distance round the trail?

Let's investigate

Make up your own trail. Put on 5 places A, B, C, D, E.
Make A to B twice as long as from B to C.
Make C to D 3 times as long as from D to E.
Make E to A half as long as from A to B.
Mark on some distances in m or km.
Write some questions for a friend and make an answer card.